YORKSHIRE
WIT & WISDOM

FROM OLD AMOS

DALESMAN

Dalesman Publishing Company Ltd
Stable Courtyard, Broughton Hall,
Skipton, North Yorkshire BD23 3AE

First Published 1996

Reprinted 1999, 2002

Text © Pete Lindup 1996

A British Library Cataloguing in Publication record
is available for this book

ISBN 1 85568 107 2

Printed by The Amadeus Press Cleckheaton, West Yorkshire

MORE
YORKSHIRE
WIT & WISDOM

FROM OLD AMOS

INTRODUCTION

My father's creation Old Amos first appeared in Dalesman just as Britain was entering its second Elizabethan Age. Man had ascended Mount Everest but had not yet walked in space. We still had imperialism, trams, rationing, variety theatres, gas lamps, whip and tops, horses and carts, Gaumont cinema and Picture Post. Television had one black and white channel. A suit of clothes could be purchased for less than it now costs to dry clean. Micro-chips were 'scraps' from the fish-shop. An Eagle comic could be swapped for two Film Funs and there were still shepherds where the M62 now runs.

Though, in an ever-changing world, one thing has remained constant: the foibles of everyday life. Our struggle to understand, tolerate, ignore or just laugh at the passing scene is as vital today as it was in coronation year.

This new collection of the Old Codger's comments will hopefully bring forth the same smiles, philosophical nods or even a laugh or two as they have in the past. As Amos himself might say, "A smile costs nowt — so it's money well spent!" Ready? Start chuckling...

Pete Lindup 1996

"When tha's young thi looks for greener fields.
When tha's old tha can't mow what tha's got."

AH RECKON...

"Worry never changes owt except t'fellah doing t'worrying."

"They reckon that as you grow old you forget things but I can't remember ever forgetting owt!"

"They tell us that computers can do all our thinking. What we really need is a machine to do all our worrying."

"T'world looks brightest from behind a smile."

"If somebody offers thi t'world on a silver plate, tha's better off tekkin' t'plate!"

"T'world seems to be divided in two, them as do things and them as gets t'credit."

"If all t'world's a stage it could do wi' more rehearsal."

"Tha 'as to take t'world as it is and not as it should be."

"If t'world laughs at thi, laugh reight back — it's just as funny as tha is!"

"There's allus been a good crop o' food for thought but rarely enough enthusiasm to 'arvest it."

"Tha can warm to others best if there's a fire in thissen."

"Foolishness is like zest wi'out knowledge."

"Tha's only young once, after that tha just thinks tha is."

"Do you remember t'days when fowk would do wi'out owt they couldn't afford?"

"When I were young, little lasses liked painted dolls, little lads liked soldiers, then when they grew up it were t'other way round."

"A word o'advice to young men: Don't tell thi girlfriend that tha's unworthy of 'er — let 'er find out for 'erself!"

"Tha's only young once, t'trick is to make it last as long as tha can."

"Things were so dull in t'old days, t'favourite pastime were yawning."

"Best time o'life was when tha were young enough to know everything."

"If tha can't think of a snappy reply a yawn works just as well."

"Yawning is opening thi mouth and wishing others would shut theirs."

10

"Character is what we acquire when youth and good looks start to fade."

"There are two things we all worry abaht — yesterday and tomorrow."

"Don't waste time worrying abaht thi station in life, there's allus somebody to tell thi where to get off."

"Ah reckon that t'only person who can afford to worry is t'one who doesn't need to."

"Tha can allus find an excuse if tha's weak enough to need one."

"Ah reckon some folk's weakness is t'strongest thing about 'em."

"Tha can allus tell an egoist, but tha can't tell 'im much."

"T'only way to end up wi' a small fortune is to start wi' a big 'un."

"Conceit is most often caused by 'I' strain."

"Everybody 'as perfect eyesight when it comes to seeing t'faults in others."

"We can all see farther than we can reach — but that doesn't stop us reaching."

"If tha's money thi can buy all t'friends tha wants. But are they worth it?"

"Never worry abaht what people think of thi. They probably don't anyway."

"There are folk who don't know what's right. There are folk who don't know what's wrong — and lots more who don't know t'difference."

"Give credit where it's due — most folk are living on it anyway."

"It's nice to 'ave a 'oliday and get away from everything, except t'expense."

"Some fellah may take a 'oliday to get away from 'is problems. Others take their family wi' 'em."

"Don't tell a tired looking chap 'e needs a 'oliday 'e might just 'ave 'ad one."

"Some folks are not actually liars, they just tell t'truth in such a way that tha doesn't believe 'em."

"If tha wants to annoy somebody, tell lies abaht 'em. To aggravate 'em, tell t'truth."

"A lie can travel all round t'village while truth is still putting its boots on."

"Travel can broaden thi mind but it can also flatten thi finances."

"It's good to 'ave a change. Even if it's only doing nowt somewhere else."

"Ah reckon t'difference between conversation and gossip is, one exercises t'mind and t'other exercises t'tongue."

"T'easiest way to cut thi own throat is wi' a sharp tongue."

"Funny 'ow a dull mind and a sharp tongue often go together.'

"Pipe smokers are seldom trouble makers. They spend so much time cleaning it, filling it and trying to keep it lit they've no time for owt else."

"Ah can't decide if saving money is unfashionable or just impossible."

"More and more food is frozen these days, and

that includes food for thought."

"T'best way to keep going is to keep taking on new thoughts and throwing out old habits."

"It can take a lot o'big words to cover up a small mind."

"Ah reckon it's better to be in debt than be one of thi creditors.

"It's best to keep thi temper — nobody else wants it."

"When tha's in t'right tha can afford to keep thi temper. When tha's wrong tha can't afford to lose it."

"T'most amazing thing abaht somebody being

"My advice to a lad who wants to get on, is this — start courtin' boss's daughter."

arrested for disturbing t'peace is that they found any to disturb."

"If tha's got an axe to grind be careful tha doesn't fly off t'andle."

"Some folk are 'ard to fathom. They spend money they 'aven't got to buy things they don't need to impress people they don't like."

"If tha gets carried away wi' thi own importance tha'll not 'ave so far to walk back."

"'Aving a lot o'brass doesn't make thi polished."

"It isn't only t'quiet folk who don't say much."

"I've allus preferred being a pedestrian to a driver. For one thing it's easier to find a parking space."

"Why do town folk call it t'rush hour when t'traffic's at a standstill?"

"A sharp tongue sometimes leads to a split lip."

"There's allus two sides to an argument but seldom an end."

"Digging for t'truth is better exercise than jumping to conclusions."

"There's nowt spoils a good rumour better than a few facts."

"Don't give up 'cos you think you're a failure 'til you find out 'ow close you are to success."

"Ah reckon it's easier to believe a lie tha's 'eard a thousand times than a truth thi 'asn't 'eard before."

"There's no short cut to success but there's lots of trap doors to failure."

"No person is a failure as long as they can be an example to others."

"If tha thinks tha's missing t'target 'appen tha's just aiming too low."

"Tha'll never achieve owt by not doing what tha's told — or by doing nowt else either."

"It's easy to boast that tha's nivver failed to do what tha's set out to do if tha's nivver done owt."

"What we need today is more people planting beans and fewer people spilling 'em."

"It's a lucky farmer who can raise a good crop of offspring."

"Tha'll never plough a field by turning it over in your mind."

"T'young generation's all reight — especially if tha's a member of it."

"A farmer raises crops but a 'gentleman' farmer raises 'is 'at."

"T'most dangerous crop you can sow is a few wild oats."

"A man who 'as faults 'e doesn't know about 'as never 'eard 'is wife talking to t'neighbours."

"At this time o' t'year it's better to enjoy t'breet days than brood over t'dark uns."

"If tha's only got a few faults — make best of 'em."

"It's 'ard to weigh t'faults of others wi'out leaning on t'scales.

"It's easier to put your faults behind you than it is to face them."

"T'easiest way to break a habit is by dropping it."

"Changing a habit is like climbing stairs, it

were easier to do when we were younger."

"Ah reckon we all need bad 'abits, otherwise there'd be nowt to give up when we weren't feeling so well."

"I'd hate to give up bad habits and feel no better for it."

"What can thi get today wi'out money? Debt I suppose."

"I know lots o'fellows who get big cars — t'first thing they run into is debt!"

"They say that crime costs us millions a year. Ah suppose we get a lot for our money."

"It says here that a man is knocked down in London every five minutes. Poor fellow."

"If tha's got a lot to boast abaht thi doesn't need to."

"I reckon they should spend more money educating
parents and less on amusing t'children."

"Going to church can change a man, providing 'e can change a pound on the way."

"Funny 'ow when you dial a wrong number on t'phone, it's never engaged."

"'Ave you ever noticed that folk who snore t'loudest are allus t'ones who fall asleep t'first?"

"T'chap who boasts of 'aving an open mind might only 'ave a vacant one."

"If tha thinks tha's too old to set a bad example, try giving good advice."

"Sympathy is an 'andy thing to give people if tha's skint."

"There's allus summat tha can do better than anybody else — even if it's only reading thi own 'andwriting!"

"Ah reckon that asking daft questions is preferable to making daft mistakes."

"Some chaps are so proud o'themselves — they're allus letting off esteem."

"It's better to count thi blessings than magnify thi problems."

"We all want progress providing we can 'ave it wi'out change."

"Politicians are people who stand for t'country and 'ope that t'country will stand for them."

"Most o'these politicians seem to spend 'alf their time making promises and t'other 'alf making excuses."

"Ideals are like old furniture, all right to show off but too fragile to use."

"Ah reckon that some o' these 'ere politicians are too concerned wi' deals and not enough wi' ideals."

"What we all could do with are more o'them things that money can't buy."

"Nowt disappears quicker than a new idea in a mind that's closed."

"A chap wi' nowt on 'is mind is less boring than a bloke who's only got one thing."

"*Tha'll nivver know who thi friends are if tha
misplaces thi Christmas card list.*"

*"The first of April. That's the day that reminds
a lot of us what we were on the other 364."*

"It's best to keep thi feet on t'ground — even
better to keep 'em moving."

"They reckon that in ten years time there'll be

twice as much traffic abaht. So, if tha 'as to cross t'road, tha'd best do it now."

"It's easy to take a day off but not so easy to put it back."

"Some folk say 'Make thissen at 'ome' in such a way that makes you wish you were."

"Manners is summat that's never noticed until tha forgets 'em."

"Nowt is as desirable as summat tha can't 'ave."

"Ah reckon more people get knocked down by a fast tongue than a fast car."

"If young folk want to see 90 they'd better not look for it on a speedometer."

"Some o't'dresses these young lasses wear these days! Ah've seen more cotton in a bottle o'Asprins!"

"Youngsters are all right if they're given a free 'and. Providing it's given in t'reight place."

"Youth is t'time o'life when we stop answering questions an' start questioning t'answers."

"Ah reckon a bachelor is a chap who never makes t'same mistake once!"

"A bachelor is like a good washing-up liquid. 'E should work fast an' not leave rings!"

"It often puzzles me what un-married fellahs do for aggravation."

"I've allus tried to resist temptation in t'opes that a better one might come along."

"Ah reckon that t'shape tha's in depends on what tha takes two of at a time — stairs or pills!"

"It's a patient man who can keep 'is shirt on while getting summat off 'is chest."

"Some folk are that shifty they could follow you into a revolving door and come ahrt first."

"Funny 'ow politicians never seem to say owt, then insist that they've been misquoted."

"T'best 'elping 'and folk 'ave is t'one at t'end o' their arm."

"We all want to know what our politicians

stand for and they want to know what we all fall for."

"Ah reckon a politician's promises go in one year and ahrt o't'next!"

"Germs attack t'weakest part o't'body. That will account for so many 'ead colds, ah reckon."

"Ah suppose it's 'ow tha look at things. If tha not feelin' so bad tha probably not so good either."

"My doctor reckons that to keep 'ealthy ah should walk five miles a day. At that rate ah'll be at t'other end o't'country in six months!"

"If we could see ourselves as others see us we wouldn't bother to look."

"T'doctor says I've got t'body of a twenty-year old. A twenty-year old what 'e didn't say!"

"Ah suppose ah could keep fit by touching me toes. T'trouble is, I 'aven't seen 'em for twenty years!"

"Ah reckon ah'm in as good a shape as t'world's in. Come to think of it ah'm in a similar shape to it an'all!"

"Fowks used to think that t'world were flat, then they thought it were round. These days it tends to look crooked."

"If t'world laughs at thi, tha might as well join in t'joke."

"They reckon that in this world there are no two people alike. That's good news for both of 'em."

"They say that paper money is covered in germs. Luckily none of us 'old on to it long enough to catch owt."

"Allus try to learn by thi mistakes — then tha can repeat 'em as often as thi likes."

"Being tired or being lazy depends on whether tha's done a job or tha's a job to do."

*"There are three types o'chaps in this world;
t'intellectual ones, t'handsome ones and
t'majority of us."*

"Time is t'most precious thing in t'world — yet few fowk value it."

"Why does a narrow mind and a wide mouth allus seem to go together?"

"Ah reckon we wouldn't worry so much abaht what people thought of us if we realised 'ow seldom they do."

"One o't'best inventions in t'world must be newspapers. Wi'out 'em we couldn't swat flies, wrap fish or avoid seeing a woman standing on t'bus."

"A temper is one o't'few things that improves the less it's used."

"It's 'ard to give some folk t'benefit o't'doubt when there obviously isn't any."

"T'biggest fool is t'one who insists on arguing wi' a know-all."

"If you 'ave a chip on your shoulder it could develop into a heavy load."

"These 'ere modern diets are strange. Tha's expected to lose pounds by spending pounds."

"T'easiest way to tell a flower from a weed is to pick it. If it grows again it's a weed."

"It's allus amazed me 'ow roses smell so nice, considering what they've been standing in all their lives."

"There's one sure way of ending a drought — water thi garden. Then it's bound to rain."

"I can nivver find owt in my 'ouse. I 'ave a place for everything but I allus put it somewhere else."

"Tha can't improve on nature, unless tha can get it to look at the pictures on seed packets."

"T'best time for a chap to learn is after 'e thinks 'e knows it all."

"Don't kids grow up fast these days? Their voices seem to break afore they've learned to talk."

"Tha'll never get loose change from a tight fist."

"Some fowk think they should 'ave t'world. But if they got it where would they put it?"

"I don't know who deserves t'most sympathy these days, them that's 'omeless or them wi' a mortgage."

"Me next door neighbour 'as just come back from 'is first trip to London. 'E said he won't go there again unless it's moved somewhere quieter!"

"I reckon some fowk are never closer than when they're comparing ailments."

"Ah reckon t'best way to beat enemies is to make 'em your friends."

"I know a farm labourer who guarantees to give you an honest day's work. T'only trouble is it takes 'im a week to do it."

"A woman, collecting for a jumble-sale asked

me what I do with my old clothes. 'Simple,' I told her, 'I put 'em on in t'morning and I take 'em off at night!'"

"If tha can tell t' difference between good advice an' bad advice, tha doesn't need advice."

"Odd isn't it? When Ah wor a lad Ah wanted to be a man o' leisure — nah I'm a man o' leisure, Ah want to be a lad!"

"There's lots o' things money can't buy — includin' what it used to."

"Tha can get through life wi' bad manners, but it's easier wi' good uns."

"There's one good thing abaht bein' poor — it costs nowt."

"A laugh at your own expense costs nowt."

It's t'person 'at works when there's nowt to do who gets to t'front."

"Have ya noticed, summat? Years are getting shorter — and t'days longer."

"T'best way to make thi money go far is to invest it in a first-class stamp."

"Ah can't mek out t'words o' these modern songs — and I can't remember t'words o' t'owd uns."

"T'best things in life may be free — but how many of us can afford t'best?"

"Ah reckon that ambition is summat tha' as afore realisation sets in."

"T'only travellin' I do is crossin' t'channels on mi TV."

"'E 'at ceases to be a friend, nivver was a good un."

"Some fowk can't cement a relationship — t'best they can manage is a bit o' pointing."

"T' best thing to do with advice is pass it on — tha'll nivver find a use for it thissen."

"T'best way to save daylight is to use it."

"Ah'm tekkin' mi pension to t' bank — it's too little to go on its own."

"If at first tha doesn't succeed, find out 'ow much tha gets for bein' t'loser."

"Ah must be gettin' owd — it's take mi all day to remember t'name o' somebody Ah've been trying to forget all mi life."

"It's better to 'ave nowt to do than to do nowt."

"If some fellahs 'ad two 'eads, they'd still disagree wi' each other."

"It's easy to keep thi temper if t'other feller's bigger than thee."

"Don't try to meet trouble 'alfway — it can travel faster than thee."

"If I knew exactly when a piece of junk became an antique I'd be a rich man."

"If tha ever feel ashamed abaht t' way tha lives, don't hesitate; give it up — feelin' ashamed ah mean.

"He 'at knows nowt, doubts nowt."

"It costs a fortune to save money these days."

"T'trouble wi' Christmas is it's on thi afoar tha's finished paying for t'last un."

"A good education shows us 'ow little other fowk know."

"Think twice afore speakin' — it'll gi' thi chance to think o' summat more aggravatin' to say."

"Is tha like me? Able to fend for thissen as long as somebody gives thi an 'and?"

"T'best time to start a task is when tha's not in t'mood — tha'll mek a better job if it."

"Some folk wake up to find thersens famous. Others find thersens famous then wake up."

"It's not so much keepin' thi mouth shut — it's when tha does it that counts."

"Rent man is t'most popular chap in t'village. Fowk are allus askin' 'im to call again!"

"Tha knows what an 'ousing estate is? That's where they cut all t'trees dahn an' name t'streets after 'em."

"Are you like me? Get up in t'mornin' wi' nowt to do — and at bedtime there's still 'alf on it undone?"

"T'big advantage of 'aving nowt to do is tha can start whenever thi wants."

"It's not how far you go in life, but how you get there."

"Try not to be down 'earted cos t'years are passing by — be grateful that they keep turning up."

"To make a fool of 'imself a man needs only one thing — an opportunity!"

"If ignorance is bliss why aren't there more
happy people?"

"Funny thing abaht t'cold weather — a car won't start runnin' and a nose won't stop!"

"Retirement's alreight — but I wouldn't like to do it for a living."

"There's only one way to make t'budget balance — tilt t'country."

"Some folk spend hours telling thi 'ow much they have to suffer in silence."

"Tha'll never get rid of a bad temper by losing it."

"I've never been led into temptation — I've always found mi own way!"

"The only good thing on TV these days is me bowl o' fruit!"

"Ave ya noticed? Everybody knows what's wrong wi' t'world except them as can do summat abaht it."

"Women 'ave two topics o' conversation — 'ow slim they used to be, an' 'ow slim they're goin' to be!"

"First rule o' successful gardening — plant thissen in a comfy chair."

"One good thing about a bore — 'e never talks about anybody else!"

"I allus try to save mi money, cos someday it might be valuable again!"

"Ah've come to t'conclusion that it's no good finding a greener pasture when tha's too old to climb t'fence!"

"If thi can be alone wi' thi thoughts tha's in good company."

"Ah've allus liked silence — ever since Ah first 'eard it!"

"'Ave ya noticed 'ow some fowk are like blisters — they only appear when all t'works done?"

"Ah reckon a man who's in love wi' 'imself should get a divorce."

"Christmas is the time to remember the past and 'ope nobody forgets thi present!"

"Ah reckon one o' t'reasons why women live longer than men is because they don't 'ave wives."

"Memory is a useful thing, wi'out it
we'd 'ave nowt to forget with."

"Ah bet if we all 'ad a magic lamp there'd be a tax on genies!"

"A lot of folk run out o' conversation afore they run out o' words."

"In our village a fellah is known by 'is first name — and his last scandal!"

"A chap who thinks 'e knows it all 'as merely stopped thinking."

"These days Ah reckon there's no such thing as an idle rumour — they're all busy!"

"Intelligence is like a stream — when it's deepest it makes less noise."

"Some fellahs can give up smokin' and drinkin' — but they can't give up tellin' you abaht it!"

"Tha can't buy friendship wi money, but tha can make enemies if tha's too much of it."

"Tha knows when a fellah is in t'reight if 'e admits 'e's wrong."

"If it pays to be ignorant there would be more rich people around."

"T'bloke who thinks 'is wife can't take a joke is overlooking t'fact that she probably married one."

"Some women look for an ideal 'usband, others look for a single man."

"Our language is called the Mother Tongue. Probably because father seldom gets a chance to use it."

"I can read any foreign language — providing it's printed in English."

"Some folks lead such dull lives, they count sheep to keep awake."

"Most folk today seem to use sign language — they sign for this and they sign for that..."

"Not all men are homeless, it's just that some are at home less than others."

"Some women insist that all men are alike. Well, I suppose we are — we're all different."

"Ah reckon it's better to 'ave nowt to remember than 'ave nowt to forget."

"Any fool can go to bed, but it takes a man to get up these mornings."

"I've allus 'ad a good memory — it's just too short."

"Some o' these modern lasses don't wear

lipstick. That's 'cos their mouths are not still long enough for 'em to put it on."

"T'only exercise some folk get is letting their mind wander."

"T'best way to change a woman's mind is to agree wi' 'er."

"I've got enough money to last t'rest o' mi life — unless I spend some of it."

"They say that tha can't take it with thi — most of us can't even afford to go!"

"There's so much debt in the world, some folk won't even pay attention."

"Ah think t'old songs are better than new uns. They 'ad words tha's forgotten instead of ones tha can't understand."

"If folk want thi opinion they'll usually give it to thee."

"Some folks make poor neighbours, they keep taking back everything tha borrows from 'em."

"Tha allus know when summer 'as ended, thi neighbour brings thi lawn mower back."

"Everybody knows more than somebody else but nobody knows more than everybody else."

"If everybody was somebody that would mean that nobody was anybody."

"'Ave ya noticed that people our age are a lot older than we are?"

"It's an unhappy woman who knows a secret that nobody wants to know."

"Some folk 'ave found a sure-fire way to save money — they use other people's."

"Save up, get by wi'out what tha need and then tha can afford summat tha can do wi'out."

"We were so poor when I were a lad I could only afford one measle at a time."

"People tell me I carry me age well. So I should, I've 'ad years of experience."

"Does tha think that wrinkles are hereditary? If so I must 'ave given me parents a few!"

"Grandparents are very simple — even a child can operate them."

"Whether a man gets married or remains single 'e'll live to regret it."

"Ah reckon that t'reason a woman isn't married to t'same man for long is because 'e isn't t'same man for long."

"A chap might be a poor 'usband but at least 'e used to be a rich bachelor."

"If thi must borrow owt, borrow from a

*"If somebody complains that it's raining ahrtside just
remind 'em that it's better than raining inside."*

"A pound goes a long way these days. Tha can carry one around for weeks afore tha finds summat it'll buy."

pessimist they won't expect it returning."

"A luxury only becomes a necessity if thi neighbour 'as it."

"A young lad asked me if there were pop songs when I were young. "Well," I said, "There were 'Pop Goes T'Weasel'

"Ah wonder if this 'ere modern music is as bad as it sounds?"

"I only know two songs by 'eart. One is 'Ilkla Moor Bahr Tat', and ah think t'other one is as well!"

"Try not to spend most o' thi time wondering 'ow to spend most o' thi time."

"If a father wants to regain 'is youth 'e should 'ide the lad's car keys."

"If a young woman wants to keep 'er youth she'd better not introduce 'im to anybody."

"These days nothing is impossible, in fact lots o' folk do nothing for as long as possible."

"If tha wants to keep thi children out of 'ot water — put some dishes in it!"

"Some o' these modern youngsters are in 'ot water so often tha'd think they were tea bags."

"It costs more to amuse a child than it does to educate it."

"It takes a lot of hard work to relax today."

"T'best birthday gift tha can get is money. It's easier to change than a present."

"A mealtime is when t'young uns continue eating, and sit down to do it."

"Funny 'ow rain makes flowers grow and buses disappear."

"One good thing abart rain — tha doesn't 'ave to shovel it."

"Tha knows tha's reached perfection when fowk stop talking abaht thi."

"Tha can't judge a man by 'is manners if there's not enough evidence."

"Allus speak well of thi enemies, after all, it were thee who made 'em."

"A barber is one o' t'few people who can talk behind thi back."